Happy Tuesday!

A Guide to Coping with Depression and Anxiety as a
High School Girl

Anna Shutley

To Mom, thank you for diving headfirst into this season of my life. Thank you for deciding to stand with me and face this, and for all the sacrifices you made to do so. You are my very best friend.

To Dad, Mark, and Caroline for keeping me sane and for loving me throughout all of my tumultuous moods. I thank God every day that he put me with y'all. Thank you for not seeing me as broken even when I thought that I was, and for continuing to make me feel important and loved unconditionally, always.

To Ansley, for being my rock. No matter how many times I fall you give me the same encouragement to get back up. You fill my life with joy.

To Andrea and Jamison, for making me laugh when I never thought I would again.

To Benny, thank you for being my biggest cheerleader. It was a privilege to be your best friend.

To Emma, for telling me that it was okay to be transparent about my feelings. Your strength is inspirational, and you give me the words to say what I need to. Thank you for always encouraging me to grow and live a life that I love. I'm my best self when I'm with you.

To Donovan, for dropping everything to help me through my panic attacks. I am so grateful for the way that you accept me.

To Becky, for keeping me alive and showing me the light at the end of the tunnel. You were right about everything.

To Liz and Kia, because nights with you erase years of pain. Thank you for being my home away from home and making me feel safe and loved.

To Larry, Drew, and God's Farm, for healing my soul, showing me my purpose in life, and for leading me to the rock that is higher than I when my heart is overwhelmed.

To Christian, you ground me and keep me focused on what's important, and reminding me to embrace the process of figuring everything out.

To Colman, for showing me that my depression was no longer my story. Your philosophy of positivity is my favorite thing about you. I am so lucky to have you in my life.

They say it takes a village, and you are mine. Forever grateful.

Foreword

The second semester of my sophomore year of high school started off with a bang; a diagnosis of clinical depression and anxiety that left me wondering, *okay, what now*? The diagnosis made sense; leading up to this moment in my therapist's office had been months of panic attacks, being unable to talk to adults on the phone, nights curled up in a ball crying on my floor, and thoughts of suicide.

"Am I going to be on these antidepressants forever?"

"Definitely not. This a season of your life. It's an incredibly painful one and you're going to have to work hard to get out of it, but it's just a season. Life won't always be like this" my therapist responded.

Maybe you're like me and step one was leaving the doctor's office, picking up your prescription, and heading immediately to Barnes and Noble for some wise words of those more experienced than myself. However, most of these books came up short. Sure, this middle-aged psychologist knows what he's talking about, but he doesn't understand what it's like to be a teenage girl battling demons in her head every day. I'm hoping this book will provide a different angle. You don't want to be told "It'll get better" and neither did I. So here is what I have learned, no beating around the bush or empty advice. I hope it helps.

I am not a professional, and you should take this advice with that in mind. I am speaking from personal experience and what has worked for me in my battle with depression.

The suicide hotline is 1-800-273-8255. There is also a Crisis Text Line, available if you text "NAMI" to 741-741.

A Few Basic Facts About Depression

The biology of depression.

Depression is caused by a depletion of serotonin in the brain, the chemical that affects mood and behavior, as well as sleep, memory, and appetite. Because this neurotransmitter affects mood, a lack of it can cause the feelings of sadness, hopelessness, and depression. Depletion of serotonin can be caused by prolonged periods of stress, digestive issues that slow the breakdown of food and prevent serotonin production, lack of sunlight, poor diet, and hormone changes and imbalances.

It is a mental illness.

What is most important to remember is that depression is a disease. Just like any other disease, it comes with a diagnosis, has some pretty crappy side effects, and many people deal with it their entire lives.

There is not always a definitive cause for the disease.

You don't have to have a childhood trauma or a difficult life to be affected by depression. Depression is a disease that has the potential to debilitate anyone. There is no reason to feel guilty about your mental illness just because you have a stable life.

Side effects.

Side effects of depression are very subjective to the individual. Some of them include; constant fatigue, an unshakeable sadness, lack of motivation, lack of energy, disinterest in usually exciting activities, an inability to see a positive future, and thoughts or actions of self-harm or suicide.

You feel everything intensely.

Most people with depression feel their negative emotions very intensely, but more often than not they experience every other emotion of the same caliber. When I'm sad, I'm devastated. When I'm angry, I'm fists-clenched furious. When I'm happy, I can't contain my joy. I experience emotions on a more dramatic pendulum than the average person, and sometimes I wish I could take a break for a moment and not feel anything. However, at the end of the day, I have come to appreciate my emotions. I want to experience as much of my life as possible, be that in the severity of my feelings, or in anything else.

The bad episodes end, but they're not gone, they're waiting for you to be vulnerable again.

It took me a long time to learn that depression comes and goes in waves. Occasionally I would have a really good day. I'd wake up so happy and energized and would write down inspirational quotes and have so much clarity about my mental illness. My inner voice would think "Wow, I'm recovered! Every day from now on will feel this good". Inevitably I would be shattered when the next morning I woke up and the euphoria was gone, leaving me down and listless. The darkest days also came and went, usually arriving without warning or explanation and knocking me off my feet for a while. These days were humbling and reminded me that I was still fighting a hard battle. It was frustrating because of how back-and-forth I would feel, and it was always a reminder in the back of my head that even if I was having a great day, it wasn't going to last. The flip side of that is that the worst days or periods of time don't last either. Don't generalize how you feel and let the presence of a dark day convince you that the good days never existed at all. They did exist, and there will be more of them, right around the corner.

Everyone experiences depression differently.

Depression manifests itself differently in everyone. For some people, it's like a dull ache; it gets in the way occasionally and is a constant reminder in the back of one's mind, but doesn't prevent them from doing most things. For other people, depression is debilitating in the form of not being able to get out of bed, even to eat or shower and being physically unable to do anything. If you are anywhere on this spectrum, it is possible that you are struggling with depression. The critical thing to remember about depression is that it's not a contest. If your depression is relatively mild and you are still able to function in school/work/life in general, your pain is still *so* valid. You don't have to pretend like you aren't in pain because "others have it worse." Others will always have it worse and others will always have it better. You would never tell someone, "You really shouldn't be happy, because there are so many people out there who have it so much better than you," so why do people say that for sadness? You would never tell someone with a broken arm to not go to the hospital because "it could be so much worse." Mental illnesses should be dealt with and taken as seriously as physical illness and injury. If you are in need of help, it is okay to seek it, and it is okay not to be okay.

Reminders for Anyone with Depression:

Your illness does not define you.

When I was first diagnosed with depression, I lost a massive element of my self-identity, and the depression seemed to take over. I began doubting everything; why am I laughing if I am depressed? It consumed me. I became The Depressed Person. That was the first and foremost element of myself, and everything else was secondary. You need to remind yourself that you are not a Depressed Person, you are a person with depression. If you try to think in this mentality, you can regain control of who you are. Your depression does not define you. You have depression, but you are so much more than that. A person with depression is still a person above all else.

One of the biggest mistakes that I made during the worst of my mental illness was letting my depression be the most defining characteristic of myself. Everything in my life started to fade in the presence of this parasitic mental illness. Whenever I had conversations with people that extended beyond small talk, I brought up my depression or changed the conversation to include it. I made huge proclamations about my illness to everyone I considered even sort-of a friend and felt like no one knew me if they didn't know what I was going through. Telling the people closest to you is a good thing because it will help them to understand why you're acting differently and will help them to be a proper support system. However, it is not necessary to tell everyone about your mental illness. When you do this, you are far more likely to use your mental illness as the primary element of what makes you, you. I began to believe that the depressed Anna was the real Anna. Everything else was me pretending to be okay, and Anna did not exist without her mental illness. This is *so* untrue. My depressed self was one of my many selves, but by no means was it the most important, nor was it my primary identity. My Christian self that was anchored in my faith to God was much more important. There were so many other parts of me - being a sister, a daughter, a best friend, being intelligent and hardworking, being a runner, an avid reader, a good listener, a dog lover, a health nut, all those parts of myself (the parts that still exist long after the death of my Depressed Self) faded, and I only saw myself as A Depressed Person. Do not let your depressed self be your only self, because it is not. There is so much more to you than your mental illness, and those other parts of you will still be there when you have weathered the storm of your depression and come through the other side. Try this doodle - write your name in the center of a piece of paper and around it write all the ways you can think of to describe yourself, all the different identities that you have.

It is okay to feel sad.   ˙

So many of the positivity blogs and happiness Instagram pages that I see are promoting happiness so much that they want you to never, ever feel sad. You need sadness. As weird as that sounds to a depressed person, you need the lows to appreciate the highs and to move forward with your life. We are human beings, and none of us are going to be happy all the time, *and that is okay*. Being sad is okay. Oftentimes I used to feel guilty and angry at myself anytime I got sad, like I wasn't using my strategies from therapy well enough, or that I was being selfish or irrational by letting small things upset me. This is not sustainable. Sometimes, depressed people know that doing something will make them feel better, but they can't make themselves do that. This isn't their fault. It happens. The Pixar movie *Inside Out* captures this idea perfectly. Riley needed all five of her main emotions to be who she was. Joy kept aggressively shoving Sadness out of the picture and refusing to let her influence Riley's emotions or memories. But Riley needed to be sad in order to appreciate her joy when it did come. Her sadness helped her learn who she was and what she loved, and it told her who her true friends were. You have to experience your emotions in order to let them go. You cannot just push them away and ignore them because they will eventually resurface with more aggression. Let yourself feel your sadness, anger, disappointment, and frustration, but don't hold on to it longer than you need to.

You are not a burden.

One of the worst things about dealing with depression in high school is where your support system comes from. Most high-schoolers don't truly understand depression and are too caught up in other things to be able to be 100% present when you need them to be. People suffering from depression have intense emotions and have intense needs that stem from these emotions. People who are depressed have to work harder to make themselves happy, and more often than not they turn to those around them for support. To those who are closest to you and who would do anything for you, I promise that you are not a burden. These people genuinely want to help you, and they are not rolling their eyes when a text from you pops up, sarcastically wondering what you need now. Real friends don't do that.

However, it will help your peace of mind and make you feel better if you don't solely rely on a handful of people and expect each of them to be everything to you. One of the tokens of wisdom that my mom has given me is that everyone in your life cannot be everything to you. By this, she means that you cannot expect every one of your friends/family members to be your confidant, someone who makes you laugh, someone who gives you perfect advice, and someone who you can go to with the deepest parts of your soul. You need all of these things in your support system, without a doubt, but you cannot realistically expect every person to be *all* of these things for you. Instead of blaming people for not being enough for you, or not being able to handle the complexity of you, celebrate each person for what they *do* bring into your life, rather than on what they lack. I have friends who don't give the best advice, but who always make me laugh, and that is okay. They don't need to be everything, and I love them for the joy that they bring to me. And for me, it gives me peace of mind to know that there were a few close friends who I could always reach out to in an emergency, but I wouldn't go to the same people every time. My primary sources of advice and help when I was at my lowest points were my parents and my therapist. With both my parents and my therapist, I knew that I could tell them anything and it would not affect our relationship or their vision of me and that they were always there to help me through it. Friends are amazing resources, and you are not a burden to the ones that truly matter, but your support should come from many different sources.

It sucks.

I know how it feels to be in the middle of high school with several more years ahead of you, stressed about everything, and see a very bleak future. I know. It sucks more than just about anything. But what all the adults in your life tell you is true; You are in high school. Everything is dramatic, you probably feel socially alienated, and the constant stress makes you worry that this is what life will be like forever. I promise it is not.

You are not worthless.

Don't listen to those voices in your head that try to tell you that you are a mistake, that you are a waste of space, that you aren't worthy of your friends or your family or your life. You're here for a reason. You mean something to the people around you. Don't let the disease in your head convince you of things that aren't true.

You will not be like this forever.

I thought that I would be dealing with my depression forever and that I would be on antidepressants forever. Ha! I wish I could tell my high school self where I am now. I am sitting in my living room during the winter break after my first semester of college, surrounded by my entire family and screaming over the Duke basketball game. My first semester of college was everything and more than I hoped that it would be - I formed deep and lasting friendships and joined organizations on my campus, and I feel well-liked and at home there. I left behind the toxic relationships of my high school, and I am healthier and happier than I have ever been, physically, spiritually, and emotionally. And, as of this break, I am completely off of my antidepressants. After three years of their immense and life-saving aid, I had recovered from my mental illness, learned coping mechanisms to deal with negative emotions on my own, and changed my outlook on life to the point where I no longer needed to rely on them.

I never thought I would recover. I honestly did not believe that I would live to see my high school graduation. I assumed that my depression was my identity and that I would be carrying its weight around for the rest of my life. But I'm not. Dark thoughts still pop into my head occasionally, and a string of let-downs will still leave me feeling small and low. But depression doesn't run my life the way it used to. I regained control and when it tries to slip back in through the cracks, I remind myself of what I've learned and how to fight back.

It's pretty rare to see an armadillo in Atlanta, but I know what they look like. Armadillos have a hard shell covering most of their body, and when danger presents itself, they curl up in a ball and hope that their hard shell protects them from whatever is coming, be that a predator or a car or a storm or a falling rock. They'll sit in their balled-up shape and wait until they feel it's safe enough to come back out and face the world.

Lions, on the other hand, don't curl up in a ball and wait out the storm. If you're going to try to be a lion's predator, odds are not stacked in your favor. If you mess with a lion, it'll attack you right back, because it's stronger than you and knows that.

Recovery from depression turns you from an armadillo into a lion. Sure, life still happens and nothing is perfect, but instead of letting that predator try to crush your shell, you fight back and show the predator that you're a force to be reckoned with.

It is okay to not be okay

As soon as I started going to therapy, I began to feel pressure to get better immediately. Most of this pressure was self-inflicted because I thought I no longer had an excuse. I was seeking professional help and learning coping mechanisms and beginning to work through my problems. So, every time I had another dark day, I would feel like a failure. I labored under the wildly incorrect assumption that the road to recovery is a steady and straight uphill line. Recovery, especially from a disease like depression, is a very long and very slow process. If you are trying to achieve a life with zero dark days, you never will. Even the most mentally healthy and balanced people have bad days, days where they feel exhausted and defeated and somewhat hopeless. Sadness is a normal human emotion, and we need it.

Whenever I share my story about my journey with depression, people always apologize and tell me that they are so so sorry that I had to go through that. But I'm not. I am incredibly grateful for my years of suffering from depression. Before I ever experienced mental illness, I did not understand what true happiness was. My happiness each day was determined by what happened to me. I said that every day was "okay" and that I was doing "fine". I did not appreciate happiness nor did I take advantage of it or realize my control over my own. And then, when all my happiness was taken from me by a disease that I did not choose to develop, I realized just how much I had taken for granted. Now that I am on the other side of it, I am so thankful for those dark years. Without them, I wouldn't recognize the optimism and positivity with which I choose to face each day. And I am not just happy; I am overflowing with *joy*. That emotion that takes over your whole being and radiates out of you to infect everyone around you. I know how to make my own happiness, and I choose to do that, every single day of my life. When things don't go as planned or when I meet unexpected roadblocks, I don't let it ruin my day or my mood. As my friend Colman likes to say, "why would I let ten seconds of negative energy ruin my entire day?" My depression helped me to find my joy. And I still have bad days, like anyone else. There are still times when my heart feels heavy and facing my day feels like an impossible challenge, when I'd rather sleep for days than go to class or see people or eat or exercise. Sometimes people will say things that upset me and their words buzz around in my brain all day long, nagging me and making me feel slightly less worthy. But I never resent my low days or allow them to make me feel like a failure who has lost progress in her recovery. Because that's simply untrue. A few days off of running does not disqualify me from classifying myself as a runner, and nor does a bad day mean that I'm not recovered from my depression. It's important to stop those dangerous and destructive thought patterns before they spiral out of control. When you have a bad day, be gentle with yourself. Especially on the road to recovery, do not expect to progressively begin to feel better and better each day. That's not how it works and if you expect that, you will always find yourself disappointed. Celebrate your progress, and recognize and learn from your setbacks. The worst thing you can do is beat yourself up for not recovering as quickly as you had hoped.

"It will get better" is a useless mantra

I hate this cliché. I hate "It will get better". Because that doesn't help. It doesn't help when you're crying on your bedroom floor at 2 a.m. and feeling that clenching, horribly tight feeling in your stomach, unable to breathe. Telling someone in that situation that it will get better is as useless as telling someone bleeding out miles away from a hospital that they will get better. It may be true, but it does not help at that moment. But I understand that feeling. I have spent more nights crying and feeling completely hopeless than I can count. I know what it feels like to be thinking about going to school the next morning, wondering why you have to keep doing this. The days stretch on monotonously and each one feels the same. It feels like you're dying under those fluorescent lights, unable to see the sun for the eight hours that you are trapped in there. It feels like the remaining years of high school are never going to be over.

This was my thought process throughout most of high school: that all of these days are pointless. I had to go to a school with people who made me feel miserable, in an old building with no windows, constantly stressed about the amount of homework I had but also having to muster up so much strength to feel motivated to do any of it. I developed a dislike for many people around me, became disinterested in what I was learning, and I felt trapped by rules and social cues. And my picture of the future was very bleak. I saw myself attending an average college (in spite of being in the top 10 students in my class) with a bunch of people who were the same as my current classmates, engaging in senseless drinking, obtaining an average degree and marrying my college boyfriend to settle down at a house in the suburbs with a nuclear family and a 9-5 job and eventually dying of old age. I did not see the point in that life. I did not understand what I was working towards. What was the point of working so hard and being so miserable every day was if I was going to die eventually anyways and take none of this with me? I could not make a real difference in the world with my meek existence, so what was the point of even trying? My depression led me to take a thought and project it to a very negative conclusion in a very distant future. I had to learn and train myself to stay in tune with the present and worry less about the long term. It's much easier to have an optimistic view of your future when you focus on a more manageable goal of making each day happier.

I know that saying that "it will get better" is useless when you're in your darkest place and don't have the energy to lift your head off of the floor. But let me just say this; I did not see the point of carrying on. I did not want to carry on. But because of my medication, counseling sessions, the support of my family and friends, my willingness to seek treatment and use my coping mechanisms, and my faith, I was able to get through those dark days. And I am so, so, immeasurably glad that I did not hurt myself like I wanted to. Because now I am a completely different person than that 15-year-old sobbing on my floor. These days I have a smile on my face more often than not, and my best friends make me laugh so hard I cry every single day. I sit outside doing my homework, and I love being in the sun. I volunteer all the time and I love making people happy. I'm passionate about what I'm studying, and I am hopeful for what my future holds. And if I had ended my life when I thought I wanted to, I never would have seen the reward of reaching the other side of my darkness, and I would have missed out on all of these incredible Tuesdays.

Many self-help guides tell you to hold on for Christmases because that's always the best time of year or to hold on for high school or college graduation or for having a family in the future. But I don't agree with that. It doesn't help you to hold on for a holiday that happens every 1/365 days. Don't hold on for Christmases. Hold on for Tuesdays. Hear me out. I used to hate Tuesdays. They were the sibling of Mondays and just another dreary day of the school week, too far from Friday to be even remotely exciting. Now, I love Tuesdays. I love Tuesdays because they are so underappreciated. If you ask anyone what their favorite day of the week is, they'll almost always say Friday or Saturday. I've been asking this question for years and never gotten a different answer. But if you live your whole life for Fridays and Saturdays, you are wasting 5/7ths of your time wishing for something different. That is not a productive way to live or a strategy that is going to make you happy. If you wait around to be happy on Friday and Saturday, you are telling me the worst thing that you can do for your own happiness, which is waiting for happiness to *happen* to you. But if you decide to take something mundane like a Tuesday, that everyone around you views as arbitrary, and decide that that day is going to be the best damn day of your life, *it will be.*

One of the most important things I have learned from my journey with mental illness is that you do have a choice of how you live your life. There are so many things to be cynical about. The world runs rampant with terrorism, racism, and violence. People you love suffer from cancer and heart disease. Bees are dying, sea levels are rising, and plastic fills our landfills. Skin is prone to breakouts, your hair never looks as good as it does when you first left the salon, and sitting alone at lunch will ruin your entire day if you let it. But that's the thing - all of these sucky parts of any given day can only affect you if you let them. If you decide that the world is falling apart and there is a slim chance of life getting better then yes, your days are going to suck. But you have a choice, every single day, of where to focus your attention. If you decide to focus on everything miserable about the world, you will be miserable. But you also have the choice to do the exact opposite and focus on everything that, against all odds, is still so great and beautiful and remarkable about being alive. And that is why I believe so firmly in Tuesdays, and deciding to make every single day one filled with happy moments.

I decided that I didn't want to be several types of people. I didn't want to be a "waiting for the weekend" person. I didn't want to be someone who always says "I'm okay" when you ask how they are. I didn't want to be someone who started conversations with a complaint or a negative comment. I was tired of being that person. I was tired of wasting five days in between the two happy ones. I was tired of sitting around in circles with friends and spending hours talking about menial things and complaining. I was tired of being just "okay" every day that wasn't exceptionally exciting. This is how you feel when you just let life happen to you, and wait for happiness to happen to you, too. But if you take your happiness into your own hands and make a choice every day to be happy no matter what your circumstances, that is an incredible power. And I'm not saying this naively or saying that there aren't real, painful things in this world that make it difficult to carry on positively every day. I know that. One of my best friends' mom was diagnosed with cancer three separate times, and she lost her battle to brain cancer this year. When faced with losing the most important person in your life when you are 19 years old, you have every reason in the world to spend every day miserable and angry. But she doesn't. Because she decides, every morning, that no matter what, she is going to try to have a good day. She finds happiness in the small things and focuses on joy despite her foundation cracking beneath her feet. And that is because happiness is a choice. Everyone in the world has pain and sadness and feels burdened with something. But you cannot control what happens to you; your only power is in how you react to it. And once you understand where you have power and where you don't, you experience how freeing it is. All you have control over is whether you respond positively or negatively to your external environment. If you wake up every Tuesday morning and decide that this is going to be the best day of your life and you put a positive spin on everything and find joy in your daily schedule, you win. If you can get to this point, you have the power to be happy whenever you want to.

What to do to make yourself feel better

Depression is a mental illness, and for that reason, there is no easy fix. When you suffer from depression, it becomes nearly impossible to even *want* to get better. You have no energy for anything, especially changing your moods. It is so much easier to let the depression bring you down than it is to fight it. When a weight that heavy is hanging on your heart, it is no easy feat to shake it off. But there are some ways that you can be proactive about your own happiness.

Therapy

I spent two and a half years going to therapy, and I do not know where I would be without it. Being able to talk about everything I was feeling allowed me to lift the weight of it all off of my shoulders for a few hours. You should always talk to your parents (or any trusted adult) about how you are feeling because they need to know, but talking to a therapist is an essential addition to that. Therapists are educated, trained, and paid to help you with what you are going through, and you don't have to be afraid of burdening them. This additional layer of support is so beneficial because therapists offer a completely different type of safe space, independent of family and friends. It never hurts to have multiple refuges and places where you can unload your thoughts and emotions. I would always walk out of those sessions feeling just a little lighter and more hopeful. My therapist gave me amazing advice, but one of the best things about talking with her was simply having my emotions validated. Just hearing someone say "Anna, I am so sorry that you have to feel this way. It's really really hard, and you don't deserve this" makes you feel less alone.

Be honest with your parents (or any important adult in your life)

I would hesitate to tell my parents some of the things I was feeling because I was afraid that they would take me to a hospital, or never let me leave the house. I was also scared that they would see themselves as failures for what I was going through, or that somehow having a child with suicidal thoughts would make them depressed as well. But none of this is true. Your parents are adults, and they understand what pain is. You don't have to protect them or worry about ruining their vision of you as their perfect child. Your parents want you to get better, and they want to be there for you. And for your own safety, it is better to be honest with them. It took me months to be honest about how I was feeling. I knew that if I told my therapist that I was having suicidal thoughts, she would be required by law to tell my parents because I was a minor. I eventually gained the courage to tell her, and she asked me if I would prefer to inform my parents myself or have her tell them. I still could not bear the thought of having that conversation, so I asked my therapist to meet with them and tell them. In hindsight, I should not have been so afraid to communicate to my parents how much I was struggling. Having them aware of how I was feeling would have been safer. I was afraid of going to a hospital, but some nights I probably should have been in one, because it would have ensured that I stayed safe. Sometimes it can be hard to talk to your parents because it is hard to admit how severe your depression has become, but if things are going to improve, they have to know how you are feeling.

Medication

If you, your therapist, psychiatrist, and your parents/guardians think that medication would be a logical next step for you, I could not recommend it enough. I was hesitant to start taking medication because being a fifteen-year-old on antidepressants made me feel like a failure, and I wanted to be in charge of my own emotions and not have a pill control them. I wanted to be able to be happy without a drug. But the thing is, I wasn't *capable* of truly being happy at that point in my life. My depression felt like I was at the bottom of a ten-foot ditch, and the most I could do at the bottom of it was survive. I could barely even see the surface, much less reach it, and getting through each day was difficult enough, let alone getting through it with a positive attitude. Being on medication filled in the bottom three feet of the ditch and brought me closer to the surface. The medication took away the whole bottom layer of pain and sadness and made it easier for me to function like a mentally healthy person would. The best part about the medication is that it allowed me to finally have the energy and hope to start working on myself. And what is amazing about medication is that you aren't signed up for a lifetime. I was on mine for about 3 years. Leaning on the medicine through the worst of my mental illness while developing my coping mechanisms that I used in therapy to change my daily attitudes resulted in my ability to come off my antidepressants.

Journal

No matter who you are, writing your feelings out is helpful. It lets you release your thoughts from their swirling mass in your head and understand how you feel. I never really went back to read what I had written before, but it was always helpful to end my day by writing everything down, and it allowed me the peace of mind to sleep better. When I went to sleep still feeling all the negativity of my day, I would wake up feeling even worse.

Exercise

As much as you don't want to, exercise helps release stress and will make you feel better. Even if it's a ten-minute walk or stretching for a little while before you go to sleep, anything is better than nothing. Depression is caused by the depletion of the neurotransmitter serotonin from the brain, which can lead to feelings of sadness, hopelessness, and despair. Exercise, on the other hand, releases the chemicals called endorphins. These are released from the pituitary gland in the brain and send signals between neurons in the brain to reduce pain and generate feelings of pleasure, motivation, social connection, and euphoria (Domonell, Endorphins and the Truth About Why Exercise Makes You Happy). These endorphins can supplement the lack of serotonin in the brain and make you feel better, so don't skip out on exercise.

Stop dangerous thought patterns

One of the worst ways that my depression would manifest itself was in my downward spirals of negativity. "If I don't start studying for this quiz right now, I am going to fail it, and that will not only bring my grade down but it will prove that I do not know this material and then I'll fail the test on it, and then my overall grade in the class will drop and that'll bring down my GPA which is going on my college transcript and so I definitely won't get into the college that I want to…." Though frequently about school, these downward spirals would also involve me having no friends, dying alone, becoming obese, and almost every negative outcome of my future that was possible, I assumed would come true. It is so important to catch these negative thoughts as soon as they arise. Instead of letting them get out of control, as soon as you recognize yourself going down that spiral, consciously stop yourself. Turn your brain off for a moment and take a few deep breaths, and then check back in with yourself. Rationalize your thoughts; you are stressed about an upcoming quiz, but that quiz is not going to change your overall grade dramatically, and it is not going to determine anything about your future. If you do end up getting a bad grade on something, don't let it wreck you. A grade is a number, and it doesn't define you. When you really think about it, it doesn't really say anything about you at all. Or maybe your negativity is coming from an interaction you had with a friend. Instead of immediately jumping to the conclusion that you are probably going to lose that friend and then all your friends and be rejected by your entire school, rationalize that thought by telling yourself, "Okay, I had an argument with my friend, but it's able to be fixed, and one conversation will sort things out between us". Or maybe you frequently have thoughts like "I am never going to get a boyfriend, and I am going to die alone, and no one loves me" (my constant inner monologue). Try switching those thoughts to something more rational; "I haven't experienced a connection with someone in the way that I would like, but that is based on a small group of very immature boys. This means nothing about my worth or my future". I would also be prone to using these negative spirals to make huge generalizations about other people. I would overhear a group of girls gossiping and go home ranting to my mother about how everyone at my school was shallow and bitchy and how everyone my age was a miserable person and that I had nothing in common with any of them. Lovely, right? This goes back to the idea that every day is as happy as you make it. Once you start to focus on what's good about your day, about people, and about yourself, it becomes so much easier to rationalize these thoughts and stop yourself from jumping to negative conclusions. This is not to say that you need to switch every negative thought to a positive one, but just to make them more realistic. Instead of telling yourself a sad thought, like "no one likes me" and letting that become a depressed thought like "no one will ever like me," tell yourself "I am not finding a lot of people at my school who are like me, and that makes me feel lonely." This way, you're not denying yourself the right to having a negative emotion, you're just bringing it back closer to reality.

Accept your best effort

You are not a grade, you are not a number on a scale, you are not a college acceptance rate or a number of friends. You can't describe yourself in just one word, because it fails to capture so many of the complex things about you, so why would you let an arbitrary number determine who you are? Chances are, you are not an Olympian nor do you have a perfect IQ. So there is no point in expecting yourself to finish every class with a 100 or to have a record-breaking 5k time. At my high school, even the students with the highest GPA's failed the pop

quizzes in our AP World History class. And it wasn't because they didn't study enough or didn't get enough

sleep. They had prepared as best they could for the quizzes, and sometimes a 20% was the best that they could do.

And that is okay. The world did not implode, and they all went on to do great things. Sometimes you have to

accept that what you accomplished was the best that you could do, and that is the most that you could ever expect

of yourself. I am an avid runner and was on the cross-country team for all four years of high school. As soon as

every race was over and I had caught my breath, I would beat myself up over my time. I was wholly convinced

that I could have done better, despite having crossed the finish line moments before, utterly spent and finished on

empty. It is always easier to think that you could have done better, in anything, the moment you are able to rest.

No matter how hard you worked during finals week, as soon as you take a moment to relax on vacation, you start

kicking yourself for not pushing harder. But these feelings are inaccurate and should not be entertained. You

should never expect perfection from yourself. You should not expect anything but the best that you can do. One

piece of advice that my mom would always give me was that if one hard class that I was taking was my only class

and I could devote every moment of my time to studying for it, I would probably have a better grade. But the

reality of the situation was that I had seven other classes and two seasons of sports among other obligations and

the amount of time that I had left to devote to that class and the grades that I got *were still the best that I could do*

given the situation.

Talk to yourself like you would a friend

The most important piece of advice that my therapist gave me was to talk to myself like I would a friend.

If a friend came to me upset about a grade, I would never respond to him/her saying "Honestly, that was really

stupid of you. That's a terrible grade, and you are clearly an idiot, and you're not going to do well in the class.

You're probably going to drop a letter grade, and that will ruin your GPA. You definitely could have done better

on this assignment, you were clearly just being lazy." Would you ever stay friends with someone who talked to

you like that? I sincerely hope that you would not. If you wouldn't talk to a friend like that, why would you talk

to yourself like that? Accept yourself exactly as you are, doing the best that you can. Be gentle with yourself.

Take small steps to be productive each day

I hate the feeling of getting to the end of a day and feeling like you have nothing to show for it. Even if my depression was causing me to be unable to be productive, I would feel the effects of it even more by the end of the day. Some days, you are only going to be able to do the bare minimum. On these kinds of days, get out of bed and throw your sheets in the laundry. This will force you to stay out of bed for a couple of hours, and in this time, take a long shower and try to eat something. You will feel so much better when you are clean and crawling back into clean sheets than you did before. If you have a little more motivation and can manage more, start your day with a SMALL to-do list. Don't overwhelm yourself by assigning everything that needs to be done to this one day. They will get done eventually. Make yourself a manageable list of a few things that will make you feel accomplished to finally check off. You should also make a list of goals for yourself for the day, whether that's eating three full meals, going for a walk, or finding more things to be positive about throughout your day. Having these lists will help you to set a guideline for your day and make you feel more organized and prepared to take it on.

Spend less time on your phone

I know that every parent in this day and age is convinced that all of the evil in the world can be traced back to the latest model of iPhone. Technology is amazing! But like everything in life, it should be used in moderation. The root of the issue for me was that I (and I know that I am far from alone in this) would lay in bed for over an hour after I had stopped my homework and turned out my lights, staring at the blue light of my phone screen inches from my face. There were several issues with this behavior. First of all, blue light from phone screens is scientifically proven to interfere with sleep. The wavelengths from the blue light wake your brain up, which then tells your body to get up and move. When you put your phone down and immediately roll over to try to sleep, your brain is in awake mode and does not want to. The broader effects of this are that lack of sleep exacerbates the symptoms of depression and makes it even harder to have the energy to get through your day. The other issue with my late-night phone habit was that I would spend hours scrolling through the Instagram pages of beautiful models who seemed to have their lives together and had everything they wanted. I would look at photos of girls with flat stomachs and sun kissed skin and curl up into a tiny ball to hide my pale stomach rolls. First of all, the images that people put out on social media are always, always the highlight reels of their lives. People don't post pictures that they think are unflattering, nor do they post ones that showcase their own insecurities, bad days, negative emotions, or anxieties. Secondly, comparisons will never make you feel good about yourself. You cannot be the best version of anybody but yourself, and you may think that the best that you can do is not as good as the best that someone else can do. But you will never feel good about yourself if you use other people as your measuring stick for your own worth. Someone else's beauty, intelligence, and abilities do not take away from your own, and you were given the gifts that you were for a reason.

I would even suggest that you detox from social media for a while. You can choose a shorter amount of time, but after my junior year of high school I deleted all of my social media; Snapchat, Instagram, Facebook, everything. I didn't just delete the apps, I deleted all my accounts so that I couldn't just cave and re-download them after a week. I stayed off of them for over a year, and it was an incredibly helpful part of my recovery. Doing this helped me to spend less time staring at my phone screen, forced me to stop staying up late, and made it so that I was appreciating every moment as it was, instead of trying to take a perfect picture of it. Instead of working really hard to make my life look good, I was able to focus on making it actually enjoyable. It also showed me who was really important in my life and who I could really depend on. Friends who Snapchat you every day to keep your streak are nice, but if they won't put in the effort to send an actual text, they probably aren't someone to depend on for your support. (That being said, there's no need to cut them out of your life or be rude, but deleting apps like snapchat does have a way of showing who is willing to work a little bit extra to communicate with you). Patients with depression who go into inpatient therapy are forced to leave their phones behind, and I think that this tells us something about the negative effects that our phones have on us. Try a social media detox and see how it changes your life for the better.

Practice mindfulness

Another vital element that helps you create your own happiness is practicing mindfulness. Mindfulness essentially means being present in the moment and really taking into account your surroundings and your presence in them at a particular moment. This can be done in many different ways, the most popular of which include practices such as meditation, prayer, and yoga. But mindfulness doesn't have to be a big production or something you might think is reserved for hippies. Mindfulness can just mean that when you're feeling overwhelmed, closing your eyes and taking a few deep breaths to center yourself and remind yourself of where

you are. It means really taking in a moment and appreciating it in its uniqueness. I love practicing mindfulness for

the same reason I love Tuesdays - it helps you be present and take your life into your own hands, rather than

being a bystander in your own life and letting everything in life *happen* to you.

Self-love

In today's society we are constantly told that taking time to focus on ourselves is weak and selfish, and

indicates we can't handle the high intensity and responsibilities of the lifestyles that we choose to lead. You

should never feel guilty or selfish about making time to take care of yourself. This is a crucial element of mental

and physical health. Unless you spend your days writing romance novels in a hammock on the beach, you

probably are under a relatively large amount of stress each day, whether you feel the effects of that stress in a

very present way or not. You probably also are not getting enough sleep, not always eating things that make your

body feel good, and not taking enough time to let your mind and body relax, de-stress, and renew themselves for

more challenges and struggles ahead.

Here's the thing. You will always be stressed, and you will always have responsibilities and a to-do list a

mile long, so it's necessary to take time out for yourself. Otherwise, you will stretch yourself thin, and you will

cease to find happiness in the work that you do and the life that you live. Your body will be in pain and shut

down, and your moods will be low. Here are some things I suggest doing when you need some me-time, when

you're feeling down about yourself, when you feel lonely and unloved, when you're tired and stressed, sad,

happy, you could literally do this any time you want because no one can tell you what to do. Everyone needs to

take care of themselves, and no one should be ashamed of it.

1.   *Take a bath.* Splurge on a nice, scented bath bomb, turn the water really hot, turn off the lights and light

some candles. Sit and soak and relax for as long as you want. Listen to some music. Read a book.

2.   *Take a hot shower* if baths gross you out, or if you don't have a bathtub. Make sure you shampoo your hair

really well. Clean hair and being freshly showered is the best feeling in the whole world.

3. *Put on a face mask*, or a hair mask, or use a face wash or lip scrub (basically go crazy with beauty products). Pamper yourself.

4. File and clip and *paint your nails*. Toes too. If you have those foam toe separator things that's even better.

5. *Wash your sheets*. Fresh sheets and a clean self are the best combination.

6. *Do some yoga*. Yoga stretches all of your muscles out, relaxes you, and gives you a gentle but difficult workout at the same time. You don't need any skill to do a lot of the poses. Look up a quick ten-minute flow on YouTube and do it on your carpet. Bonus Tip: If you are having a panic attack, a yoga pose that will help you is Legs Up The Wall. Lie on the ground with your butt as close to the wall as you can get, and place your legs up towards the ceiling. If you have a pillow, a block, or a couple of books, place it underneath you, at the base of your spine. What this pose does is invert the normal circulation of the blood, and the gravity helps it pump faster, which allows your heart to slow down and calms your anxiety.

7. *Go for a run* or play some of whatever sport you enjoy. Endorphins make you happy, and finishing a workout is a rewarding feeling.

8. *Drink a tall glass of water*. Most people don't drink enough water. We are supposed to consume at least half a gallon of water a day. Drinking water is better for your skin, makes food taste better, rejuvenates you and gives you energy. Even if you don't feel thirsty, water will always make you feel good.

9. *Go get a haircut*. For me, getting my hair cut is my treat-my-self activity. I love having my hair washed by other people, with fragrant shampoos, and feeling lighter and fresher from the trimmed hair. You leave the salon feeling pampered and fabulous and fresh and your hair feels healthy and lovely.

10. *Go shopping* and buy yourself a cute outfit. I am a strong believer in retail therapy. New clothes are so fun an exciting, imagining all the places you will wear them, and if you're in the right mentality and in the right stores, you will feel confident and good about yourself.

11. *Go for a walk*. Get some peace and quiet, or if you live in a city, use the noise as distraction and get lost in it. Take some space.

12. *Write in a journal*. Letting all your feelings and thoughts transfer themselves on to paper will clear your mind and help you come to conclusions and decisions about things.

13. *Doll yourself up*. Take time putting on makeup, do your hair, put on your fanciest underwear and dress just to strut around your house and model in front of the mirror for yourself.

14. *Make yourself some tea* (or other preferred hot drink).

15. *Read a good book.*

16. *Watch a heartwarming/funny/old favorite film or tv show.*

17. *Put LOTS of blankets on your bed*, the softest ones you have.

18. *Treat yourself* with your favorite *comfort food*.

19. *Have a dance party* all by yourself.

20. *Call/FaceTime/Skype/Write a letter to/Text a friend.*

21. *Look up inspirational quotes* and start a collage of them for yourself.

22. *Go to the grocery store* and buy yourself a *bouquet of flowers*.

23. *Take a long nap.*

24. *Write yourself love letters*. This may seem dumb and self-centered, but it is so important. List everything that you love about yourself, what you hope and dream for yourself, and calm your own insecurities.

25. Stand in front of the mirror and *compliment yourself*.

26. *Challenge yourself* to say nothing negative about yourself for the entire day.

The bottom line is, do whatever it takes to make yourself feel calm and loved and taken care of. Never feel guilty of putting your work aside, shutting other people out (politely) and loving on yourself, because you can't love on others if your self is feeling neglected.

Advice for Imminent Needs

As good as reading a book or going to therapy or changing small practices about the way you live are, there are still times when you are in crisis, the world is falling apart, and you need immediate help. So here is a list of practical advice for what to do if it's a night when you're crying on your bedroom floor trying to come up with a reason to live.

1. If this is an extreme emergency situation (you are hurting yourself or planning to hurt yourself), you or someone who is with you needs to call 911, drive you to an emergency room, or call the suicide hotline (1-800-273-8255). If you do not want to or feel unable to talk on the phone, text "NAMI" to 741-741 for the Crisis Text Line.

2. Get somebody in there with you.

   You need to do this to keep yourself accountable and safe. I know that when you feel tempted to hurt yourself or to let the pain take over, you want to let it happen. You want to feel something. But if there is the smallest part of you that can resist this, just for long enough to call your mom (or anyone that you trust) into your room, then please, please do that. Tell them upfront what you need from them, because otherwise how is she to know? You can say something like "I just need you to hold me and not say anything", "I want to talk about it but just listen, don't give advice", "I want to talk about it and I want you to give me advice", or even "I just need you to be in here while I do my own thing and not talk", depending on what you need at that moment. If no one is home or no one is available to do this, call a friend and keep them on the line for as long as you need to.

3. Take a shower.

   Even if you end up just sitting in the tub with the shower running overhead while you cry, it can still be very cathartic and very soothing. Being clean will also make you feel better, calmer, and more in control.

4. Write down a list of all the reasons to stay alive.

   Things that make you happy now, happy memories you treasure, things you want your future to hold.

5. Avoid triggers that worsen your feelings

   I have a Spotify playlist of sad songs that always bring out those soft, slow, depressed emotions in me. But listening to sad songs while you are sad is never a good idea. If you are in a very dark place, don't worsen it by listening to sad music or scrolling through depression Tumblr pages. Fill yourself with things and people that swing your mood in the other direction.

6. Do something that helps you find zen

Once you've calmed down enough, try to do something that makes you happy. Watch a TV show that makes you laugh (my go-to is The Office or New Girl), read a book or the Bible, write in a journal or brain dump your thoughts into a Word Document, do a puzzle, play an instrument, do some yoga, go on a walk. Do something that makes you feel peaceful and connected with yourself.

7. Read your truths

At some point when you are at a high and feeling good, write down your truths. The things that you know to be true about yourself that your depressed self tries to convince you are lies. Statements like "I have friends who love and support me and who want to be there for me," "I will not suffer from this disease forever, and these feelings have passed before and they will pass again. What I am feeling in this moment is in no way indicative of my entire life", "I am a beautiful person, and I am not damaged by my mental illness," "I am smart," etc. When you're at your lowest, find these truths and read them to remind yourself that life is full of hills and valleys, and the valley that you are in right now is not permanent.

8. Go. To. Sleep.

I know you don't want to. You want to stay awake and feel your emotions, and you want to feel something, anything, and it is so hard to shut your brain off for long enough to let you actually sleep. I cannot tell you how many nights I stayed awake long after everyone else in my house was asleep, wallowing in my most negative feelings. I alternated between crying, texting my friends about how horrible I was feeling, playing my sad playlist, and scrolling through the Instagrams of all the people with remarkably better lives than myself. I wish that just a few of those times, I had gone and put my phone downstairs, out of reach, gotten ready for bed, and just let sleep win. I would never wake up chipper and in a great mood, but the sleep numbed the pain that I was feeling and lessened the intensity of my depressive episode. If you are someone who has trouble falling asleep, there are simple things you can do to try to help you, like counting on each breath you take, or relaxing every muscle in your body consciously, starting at your toes and going all the way up to your head.

Grades

Grades in high school feel like a much bigger deal than they are. It seems like your college acceptances are all riding on every single test and quiz you take, and you may be feeling additional pressure from other people, like your parents. As hard as it is, try not to focus so much on percentages and numbers. Just do the best that you can. Put in your best effort and accept whatever grades come from that. You will get into a college that is suited for you and what you accomplish in high school in no way determines the trajectory of the rest of your life. If everything else that you have going on in your life prevents you from making good grades or the best grades that you are capable of, don't panic. Making bad grades in high school is okay. The world will not implode, and you can continue to be successful no matter what. Next Tuesday will still come around and with it the reminder that you are in control of your happiness. Don't let a numeric GPA take that away from you.

Stress from school can be very overwhelming at times. Here are some tips to help you study smarter.

1. Permit yourself to take breaks, even if it feels like you have too much to do or you haven't accomplished enough to deserve one. Work for 45 minutes, without the distraction of your phone, and take a break for 15.

2. Make vocab much more manageable by making flashcards.

3. For textbook information, don't just reread - this won't help you commit it to memory. Write it down. Don't copy the entire book, but read it one section at a time, and after you've read it, summarize the most important information. Try to color code your notes by section and highlight the most essential information, or areas that already trouble you.

4. Freaking out because you've procrastinaed won't get you anywhere. Don't freak out, just take deep breaths and start on what you can.

5. Remove distractions while you're studying. It is easy to spend a lot of time on homework without actually accomplishing much if you are checking your phone every ten minutes. Leave your phone downstairs or in a different room while you work. That way, the distraction is removed, but you are also forced to get up and move around during your brief breaks, which will help you be more productive when you start working again.

6. Cut out an hour or at least half hour of time after you have finished your homework to turn your brain off before sleeping. Put the work down and get off your phone for the night, and then spend a little bit of time reading a book or the Bible, doing some light stretching or yoga, or journaling and listening to music. This will prevent you from going to bed each night feeling exhausted and overwhelmed, and removing your phone and to-do lists will help you sleep better.

7. Make manageable to-do lists. Don't write down every last thing that you have to do, because you'll get overwhelmed. Make to-do lists that you can feasibly complete in a day. When I'm very overwhelmed, I make my to-do lists in this format:

	Very Urgent	Not very urgent
Very Important		
Not very important		

This helps me to prioritize my time (completing everything in the very urgent and very important box first) and realize what it is I actually need to be doing at that moment.

8. Avoid sharing your grades with classmates and don't get involved in those post-test discussions. That will only lead to you comparing yourself to others and feeling inferior. Other people's grades say nothing about your own abilities.

9. Create graphs, mental maps, and charts whenever possible to help you organize your thoughts and see how each piece of information that you learn connects to others.

10. For the concepts that you have more trouble with, try teaching it to a friend, sibling, or parent. In doing this, you'll be able to quickly identify the gaps in your knowledge and see what you don't understand. Once you can successfully teach the information to another person, you'll know that you have it down.

11. Try to create your own test questions. Instead of just reading textbook information and being prepared to regurgitate it on the exam, try to guess what your teacher might test you on from a particular chapter and be sure that you can answer those questions. Practicing study habits like this one will make sure that you understand the information and can apply it, instead of just having memorized it.

12. Remember that, when you're being challenged appropriately, you're not going to feel smart. If school was always easy, it would mean that you weren't learning anything.

There is a photo that exists of me, lying in the grass outside the school building. I had just failed a quiz in my AP World History class, and I was walking home with my friends. The thought of what that result did to my grade in that class was swirling around in my brain like a huge, dark mass. I started screaming and crying, and flung myself onto the ground, having a panic attack that shook my whole body as I laid in the grass clutching my head. Afterwards, it took me a few minutes to collect myself and manage to get up. My AP World teacher loves this photo, and sends it out in a newsletter to parents and students every year, as an example of what not to do when stress overwhelms you.

At the moment this photo was taken, I was *miserable*. I was convinced that this grade meant that I was an idiot, that I would never be successful, and that I had ruined my GPA. I stressed at the thought of having to make up for this grade, and how to prevent it happening again. But how do you prepare for a pop quiz? I got home and ranted to my poor mother for another thirty minutes before trudging upstairs to do my homework. At this point in my sophomore year, I had patella-femoral tendonitis (essentially, knee and shin pain) that prevented me from running. Running was my primary stress relief and my escape from school. The only way to get out my anger and frustration was to pound it out on the pavement, one step at a time. The night wore on and my stress only increased. I finally came downstairs and proclaimed "Mom. I need to go for a run, or I am going to go crazy". Because it was 10 o'clock at night, she agreed as long as she could drive behind me. I laced up my shoes and made it half a mile before the pain was too unbearable to take another step. My pain and frustration blinded me, and I could not focus on anything besides the words in my head; "worthless, stupid, can't do anything right, failure, average, hopeless," to the point where I completely missed a car passing by and was inches from being hit. When I couldn't take the pain in my knees, my mom slowly pulled up behind me, and I got into the car. Without saying a word, she drove out of our neighborhood and through winding backstreets as I sobbed and shook in the seat next to her. I screamed and cried for an hour in that car, sitting in the dark. "The only thing that I can do to cope with my stress and depression is to run and God took that away from me. I don't know why he's punishing me, but I can't keep up with this. I am drowning" I wailed to my mom. She knew that nothing she could say at that moment would make me feel better, so she just held me and let me release all of my emotions.

We drove home after a while, and I collapsed into an exhausted and fitful sleep. This is what my school stress did to me. I was so anxious over my GPA and every single grade I got that there was no room for anything else in my life. School is undoubtedly important, but there is a limit to how much of your life school should take up, and I was far beyond that limit.

Your self-worth cannot, and should not ever depend on your grades. There is so much more to life than grades, and what you do in high school in no way determines what you do for the rest of your life. You can have crappy grades in high school and go on to do great things. People make mistakes. And most of the time, a bad grade is not a mistake. Sometimes, tests are just really hard. Sometimes teachers slip up and don't teach you in the best way that they could. There are so many extraneous circumstances. Just because you did not do well in your freshman biology class does not mean that you are terrible at science or that you have no hope of becoming a doctor. Practice rationalizing your thought patterns. Again, allow yourself the emotions of disappointment, but do not let them consume you. At the end of the day, you cannot expect anything more from yourself than your best effort.

Friends and Backpacks

One of the points that I want to discuss in this chapter is having friends who are also going through difficult times in their lives. My senior year of high school, I was still struggling with depression and anxiety and so was one of my best friends, another one of my friends suffered severely from an eating disorder, and another had dealt with years of emotional abuse and extreme family dysfunctionality. Having so many people close to me dealing with so many heavy issues taught me that everyone is going through something.

My analogy is this: everyone carries a backpack on their back. Some people's backpacks are very light and are easy to carry. Some people's backpacks weigh them down and are so heavy that it's almost impossible to walk. Making it through the day with that backpack on is exhausting. When you get through one day, the thought of waking up the next morning and putting it back on makes you want to never get out of bed. Some people's backpacks are a lot lighter, and they can take a few things out of the heavy backpacks and help those people lighten their load just a little bit. Some people have their own heavy backpacks on, and they want to help you with yours, but they can't take anything out of your backpack because their backpack is already full. The most that they can do for you is walk alongside you and keep you company as you struggle to carry your weight, and they can give you words of encouragement and remind you that you are not alone.

I wore a very heavy backpack for most of high school. One of my best friends also wore a very heavy backpack of her own. Where mine was weighed down with depression, anxiety, and perfectionism, hers was filled with immense challenges in her home life and dysfunctional family relationships. Our friendship was exactly what both of us needed; we listened to each other without expectations and never needed the other to fix our problems because we knew that they couldn't. To each other, we were a hand to hold in the darkness, and we never made the other feel like a burden or that she couldn't rant or cry or complain about what was going on. It is important, whenever you are reaching out for help, to tell people what you need. There were many nights when my mom would come into my room and try to talk to me, and I could not get the words out. I genuinely couldn't manage to force the words out of my mouth. So we eventually found what worked for us; she would check on me for her personal reassurance but when I needed to talk I would go to her, and I would start the conversation by saying exactly what I needed from her. My mom is a very driven person, and if you present her with a problem, she is going to try to fix it. That's simply her nature. But what I needed her to know was that the problems that I was facing were not going to be fixed with a lecture about getting out of bed, putting my phone away, and focusing on the positive. Some nights, I just needed to take off my backpack and tell her about what was inside it. She didn't need to take anything out or try to carry it for me, as much as she wanted to, because that backpack and that journey was mine and mine alone. I just needed her to understand. So I would tell her that I needed to dump out all of the thoughts swirling in my head and that she just needed to listen and hold me. Her advice is amazing, and I would always ask for it when I needed it.

I eventually started writing my parents letters when I couldn't manage to say what I needed to. When I needed to tell them about my thoughts of suicide, I couldn't find the courage to do it in person, so I wrote them letters. I did the same thing with my best friend - she and I would write to one another when we couldn't find the words, or when we could we would start with "I know you can't fix anything, I just need to tell you what is on my heart." If you are in a difficult place in your life, you do not need to take on the problems of others. However, you can still be a good friend to someone without absorbing their problems as your own.

That being said, it wasn't always easy to *not* take on other people's problems. It would hurt my heart to see the people that I loved struggling so much, and like my mom, I wanted to fix everything for everyone. But I quickly learned that while no one wants to experience pain and hardship, no one can escape it. We live in an imperfect world broken by sin and disease and violence and pain, and everyone that you know is fighting a hard battle. Life is not easy. We were never promised that it would be. But the inexistence of an easy life does not foretell of an impossibility of a *good* life. Life is hard and sad, but also wonderful. Human beings are resilient, and our uphill battles make us stronger. You cannot fight anyone else's battle for them, but your understanding of what they are going through and your own war stories can serve as encouragement. Be a light to those around you, and lifting others up will make you feel lighter as well. Just because you cannot do all things for people is not a statement of your value.

So, there are very good friends who are going through very bad stuff, but sometimes there are friends who are just bad for you. In high school, friendships are difficult because oftentimes friend groups have been set for a long time and are not receptive to much change. It is difficult to leave friend groups because everyone is in some circle, and it feels like even if you found the courage to leave, you would have nowhere to go. High school is cliquey and petty and it is easy to feel like you do not have much control over who your friends are.

However, as hard as it may be, remaining in friendships that derail you from your road to recovery is not healthy or beneficial in any way. Your behavior usually mirrors who you surround yourself with, and if all your friends do is complain about school, gossip about other people, and put a negative spin on everything, you're never going to feel positive and uplifted. You'll find yourself sucked into the trap of gossip; sliding in a quip about someone who is the current target of ridicule because it's so easy to do so. It's easy to be negative about everything, especially when everyone around you is too. It will always feel more comfortable to agree. But if you really want to change your mental pathways to become less negative, you have to change the people with whom you surround yourself.

My advice is this - I was way too afraid to leave my friend group when I had nowhere else to go, and I don't think that's necessarily bad. The familiarity of the group gave me some comfort, and I felt like I had a place to belong, but when I realized how unhappy I was, I began making small changes. I would still see my friends during school and sit next to them in class and at lunch, but I started saying no to occasional invitations to spend time together outside of school. I worked harder to reach out to other people and form more friendships, especially with people who I found to be happy and fun. By not limiting myself to the group that I was in, I realized how many people were right there in front of me but who I had never bothered to get to know better. The more I did this and the more connections I made outside my group, the more I liked them and the less I felt trapped in the negativity of my original friendships.

My middle and high school years dampened my view of friendship, and it was not until I met my high-school and college best friends that I understood how wrong I had been. These friendships are so full of joy and positivity, and they bring that characteristic out in me. They support me in everything that I do and want nothing more than for me to succeed. They always want to hear what I have to say and never make me feel like a burden or that I am damaged or broken because of my past and my history with mental illness. Surround yourself with people who have similar goals to you and who will inspire you to continue growing and evolving. You should never be content to stay where you are; be grateful for where you are but think bigger and bolder, and always strive to be the best version of yourself.

It is easy to stay in friendships that make you feel safe or that make you feel higher up on the ridiculous social ladder that exists in all high schools. But like in all things, you and your mental health come first, and the things that slow down your recovery aren't worth your time. You are FAR more valuable than that.

Boys

Like many teenage girls, I spent a large amount of my high school career wishing for a boyfriend. I pined for that attention and affection. I longed for someone to make me feel attractive because I was always telling myself that I wasn't. I was embarrassed that at 16 I hadn't had my first kiss yet. I didn't need any huge commitment; I just wanted at least something, the smallest idea that a boy could be into me. The longer I went without that, the more I struggled. And like the premise of this entire book, I am not here to feed you the lines of now high school boys aren't worth dating anyways and how you're better off without them. Because it does suck! It makes you feel like you're not good enough, you wonder what everyone else has that you don't, and then you start trying to figure out what is wrong with you. I would find everything that I hated about myself and think "It's probably this," and when I ran out of things to pinpoint, I would start noticing things that had never bothered me before. The list of insecurities got longer and longer. And it doesn't help when your friends who are dating or have dated boys try to reassure you, because no one understands how it feels to feel so unwanted. All I can do is promise you that you won't feel this way forever and that your time will come.

If you are struggling severely with your mental health, now is not the time to get into a relationship. You will inevitably put the weight of your illness on that person, and no one can carry that weight. It will put a strain on your relationship and while it can be good to have distractions, in the end, having to keep yourself accountable to another person and fulfill their needs while you struggle to fulfill your own is way too much stress. If you do find yourself in a relationship, it is vital not to let that relationship consume you. In all relationships, you need to retain your identity outside of that person. There need to be things that you are passionate about, that you spend your time on, and that make you happy besides that person, and they need to do the same. For people who suffer from depression, it can be so easy to make another person responsible for your happiness when you are unable to do so yourself. However, this is not healthy and not sustainable. You put your partner in the position of dating a person who is highly dependent on them, and they also become fearful of being honest with you or needing things from you because of the delicacy of mental illness.

You are in no way unlovable or unworthy of being loved because of your mental illness, but you must proceed with caution when you enter into a relationship with someone. You cannot be expected to deal with the weight of your mental illness alone, but neither can your significant other. This is why broader support systems that include parents, friends, therapists, etc. are so important.

It is also important to be wary of potential or current partners who are on a mission to "fix you." If someone thinks that they can cure you of your mental illness, this will lead to pressure and unhappiness. You deserve to recover from your depression, but your road to recovery and that journey is yours alone, and one that is slow and comes with many hills and valleys. No human being is going to be able to fast-track your recovery or suddenly heal your mental illness, and if it feels like they are, then you are once again coming into the dangerous territory of circumstantial happiness. Your journey must continue with or without the influence of this person. Your mental health will always be more important than any romantic relationship, and you have to be happy with yourself as you are, before you can confidently say that you'll be happy in a relationship.

If you are in a relationship with someone and you feel like you have lost your identity or they have lost theirs, if you feel trapped, or even if that relationship is simply not serving you or your goals and values anymore, it is okay to leave. Don't make the mistake of believing that you owed a boy your entire life because you are in love. Love is a beautiful thing, but it shouldn't be used to manipulate people or make them feel obligated to anything. One of my favorite pastors from my high school youth group gave this dating advice: your romantic relationship should take up 20% of your time and energy. This is still a huge chunk of your time, and there need to be other things that you are focused on. Your own mental and physical health, your relationships with family and friends, school, your activities, planning for and investing in your future, and so many more things should also be very prevalent aspects of your life.

Toxic School Environment

One of the main triggers for my depression was my toxic school environment. My school was highly competitive, and I fell into the trap of comparing my grades to others every single day. I felt like I was competing with my classmates for college acceptances and that one slip-up would cost me greatly. Everyone talked about whose GPA was a decimal point higher than everyone else's. I spent most of my years feeling like I was living in the set of Mean Girls, with constant petty drama, cliques, and being a definite part of the out-crowd. It feels superficial to talk about it, and it's slightly ridiculous that the "popular" crowd is still a thing, but it is so easy to feel alienated and alone. High school girls, especially, are the worst. I am positive that everyone reading this has experienced the pain of not being included, and the much worse feelings of being excluded by girls you thought were your friends. Teenage girls make drama out of nothing and choose to talk to everyone besides the one person that they should when small issues arise. I watched so many girls suddenly and unexpectedly get pushed out of their friend groups for basically no reason at all. It's another one of those things that just plain sucks. I don't have much advice for this besides that having a few very close friends who you can always count on will always be better than a big group, and you should find places at your school that make you feel like you belong. Make friends with people who might also feel excluded. The best part of my high school experience was my cross country team. This group of girls was so much fun to be a part of, and it was always rewarding to be working towards the state meet, accomplishing things as a team, and having people who support you to cheer you on. There are so many different sports, groups, and clubs in high school and if you can find one that makes you happy and makes you feel welcome, you should stick with that. It is also crucial to have things to do every day besides homework or school to keep you sane.

What you need to know about the environment of your school is that you are not able to change this situation. You cannot change the people that you're surrounded by, the naturally petty and dramatic environment of any high school, or the brutal eight hours under fluorescent lights. But like so much of this book is talking about, you only have control over how you react to your environment. You can choose to be a light in a toxic environment. You can choose to be a positive influence of kindness and grace among people who are the opposite. It is always going to be easier to do what everyone else is doing, to bow to the pressure of gossiping and complaining. But it will make you feel much, much better to bring a little bit of positivity to people's days.

Above all, difficult situations make you a stronger person. Weathering a challenging environment for years is going to make you a more resilient person and gives you a chance to work on your ability to be happy no matter what your circumstances are. Circumstantial happiness is fleeting, and even if you loved your school and everyone in it, that happiness would vanish at the appearance of any small discontent. There will always be times in your life when you are working with or interacting with people you would rather not, or could imagine for yourself a more ideal situation. The grass is always greener somewhere else, but if you live like that, you will always be dissatisfied. Try to work on making yourself happy exactly where you are. Throughout the day, keep a running list of every good thing that happened to you, however small. Force yourself to refrain from conversations that put down other people. Make a rule to never start a conversation with a complaint. I am not trying to convince you that your school is not as bad as you think or that someone else always has it worse. I *hated* my school for a long time, but I eventually realized that the feeling was doing nobody any good. My

negativity about school and the people in it did not inspire my classmates to want to be better people. The only

person affected by my miserable attitude towards school was myself. I felt that lump of dread in my stomach

every morning when I walked in, and I carried it around with me all day long. Every time I would pass by a group

of "popular" (I hate using that word because it feels childish or as if I'm making this up but that truly is how it

feels) girls laughing about something I would roll my eyes and tell myself that of course their lives were so much

better than mine, because they had everything and it was all easy for them. Who does this internal dialogue

benefit? Not those girls, certainly not myself. The only person that you hurt when you harbor all this negativity

and resentment is yourself. Of course you feel that knot of dread in your stomach walking in every morning

because the day before, and every single day before that one, you spent your whole day focusing on everything

that was bad about people and letting the unfortunate elements of a bad environment ruin your day. You are only

making yourself more miserable. Harboring resentment for people in your school who seem to have much better

lives than you does not affect them in the slightest, it just continues to chip away at your own self-confidence.

And reality-check, even those classmates who seem to have everything together probably don't. One of the

biggest things that I learned throughout high school was that everyone is going through something. If you want to

be different from all the monotony of personality you see within your school, then be different! But be different

by being kind and optimistic, not by further alienating yourself and convincing yourself that no one understands

you. Be open to new relationships and people who may walk into your life.

By the end of my senior year, I felt like I was always walking around in a rain jacket. The negative

comments that other people made, everyone else getting stressed and agitated about their workload and trying to

make it a competition of who had the most to do, feelings of being left out by different groups; all of that rolled

off of me like raindrops on nylon. I had gotten to the point where I stopped being a sponge, soaking up everyone

else's negativity to make myself feel heavier and sadder throughout each day. This came to me through a

breakthrough with my therapist, when I realized that I did not want to be so much like everyone else. Spoiler

alert: you are always going to have a lot of homework to do! But groaning and rolling your eyes and whining to

your classmates isn't going to make your homework go away. People are always going to say things that rub you the wrong way, and there are always going to be people that make you feel small or unwanted, or who get on your very last nerve, but I learned that letting these comments roll off of me instead of taking everything to heart was a much better use of my time. At the end of the day, no one's opinion matters except your own. Do you like who you are? Do you think that the way that you act on an average day (not your very best day) is a good reflection of how you want to be perceived? The image of yourself that you put out is not a reflection of who you say you are or who you think your ideal self is, it is based on how you act. You can be like everyone else and complain your way through every Tuesday of your life, or you can bring something different to the table and show everyone around you that the "eh" mood is not the best one.

Anxiety

The two types of anxiety that are most common are panic attacks and generalized anxiety disorder. According to the Anxiety and Depression Association of America, panic attacks are characterized as "the abrupt onset of intense fear or discomfort that reaches a peak within minutes and includes symptoms such as...accelerated heart rate, sweating, trembling, shortness of breath, chest pain, feeling dizzy, chills or heat sensations, feelings of numbness, feelings of unreality or being detached from oneself (depersonalization)". Panic attacks are often triggered by a crisis or overwhelming stress, or even something as small as a disagreement between friends or a sudden change in plans. If you suffer from panic attacks, it is important to have a plan for when they arise, especially if you are in a public place.

If you are having a panic attack at school:

1. Try to excuse yourself to go to the bathroom if at all possible.

2. Spend some time pacing the halls and walking. This will help calm your brain and expend the excess of energy that is building up.

3. Regulate your breathing with deep, consistent inhales and exhales, counting the seconds as you breathe in/out or counting the number of breaths total.

4. When you have restored your breathing to normal, try splashing cold water on your face in the bathroom or getting some to drink from the water fountain and allow yourself time to collect yourself before

returning to class. Don't hesitate to explain your situation to your teacher in private if need be - they will almost always be very accommodating and helpful, and this way they will know that you are not purposefully skipping class.

5. Download the app "What's Up?". This app has games that will help you distract yourself and calm down. It also has several pages with information about anxiety and depression and more helpful tips. I used this all the time, especially if I could feel a panic attack coming on and it was not an opportune time to leave class. You have it with you on your phone all the time and it is a lifesaver for when you need to quell your anxiety.

Sometimes, you have to let the anxiety wave ride itself out. Making plans and having coping mechanisms are always helpful, but sometimes your anxiety needs to manifest itself in your body and debilitate you for a few minutes before you can really get rid of it. One of the most important tips is to avoid anything that you know is a trigger: I love concerts, but I cannot go to them if I do not have my own seat. At music festivals or in the pits of concert arenas, there are way too many people surrounding me and too many loud noises and people touching me, I panic. So I know to avoid these types of concerts/concert seats. If I am in a crowded mall or restaurant or anywhere that my senses are being overwhelmed, and I can feel my anxiety building, I remove myself from that environment as quickly as possible, even if it is just a momentary relief of sitting in the bathroom for a few moments. Pay attention to your body and listen to its warning signs to try to prevent a full-blown panic attack.

Generalized Anxiety Disorder (GAD) is very different from panic attacks. According to the Anxiety and Depression Association of America, people who suffer from GAD experience a heightened level of stress and worry about many different things throughout each day. Living with GAD is exhausting because being constantly stressed and worrying about the possible negative outcomes of everything that you do drains your energy. It is more than just experiencing some stress before a big test or nerves before a public speech; individuals with GAD have excessive stress about everything in their lives, most commonly from finances, social events, and relationships.

Dealing with GAD is different from coping with panic attacks because GAD does not go away nor can it be reasoned with to calm down. My anxiety still affects me, primarily socially because I have always experienced anxiety about talking to new people, making extensive plans, and about whether or not my friends actually like me.

On my Accepted Students Day at my college, the president of the university gave a speech about how we are the most overscheduled, hyper-organized generation of students, and that we write into our schedules when we have time to have conversations with our parents. It is true that our generation is way too busy and that there is far too much pressure on us, but the majority of that is out of our control. In high school, you cannot change the fact that you have to be in the school building for 8 hours a day and doing homework for several more, or the fact that you have to be participating in extracurriculars and other activities to improve your college resume. That is sadly the reality of high school. However, despite the words of my school's president, it helps me to be hyper-organized. I love writing to-do lists of what needs to be done each day and marking those items off. I use a bullet journal, which I would highly suggest to anyone. Bullet journals are essentially blank dotted journals in which you can create your own planner however best fits your life. I use mine to keep track of daily events and to-dos, monthly overviews of what I need to accomplish that month, healthy habits tracking so that I can be proactive about improving my health and productivity, and a spending log to track how much money I spend. I also keep pages where I write everything that made me happy that month, which is lovely to look back on when you are feeling low.

I know I have said it before, but exercising regularly really helps keep my anxiety at bay. I love to run, but whatever form of exercise you like will help you to release your pent-up energy, produce happy endorphins in your brain. Exercise enables you to silence your anxiety for an hour, and your body and mind will thank you. The key to having exercise help you is to be as consistent as possible with it. Track (in your bullet journal! :)) how often you are exercising and set small goals for yourself each month. Don't be unrealistic and go from doing nothing to working out six days a week. Start out small and build your way up but be consistent and regular with it.

One piece of advice that I got was to treat your anxiety like it is a small child and talk to it that way. When you feel it start to build, as silly as it may sound, talk to your anxiety. "I know that this crowd is really, really overwhelming and you feel like you can't breathe. But take a deep breath - see! You can breathe just fine.

Nothing in this crowd is going to hurt you, and you are okay!" or "I know that having your teacher assign you 3 hours worth of homework makes you want to lay your head down on the desk and give up. But you have gotten through nights like this before, and it's never as bad as you think it will be. Take it one assignment at a time." This method will not only help you rationalize your thought processes and stop them from spiraling out of control, but it will help you when you disembody your anxiety from yourself. This reminds you that your anxiety is a part of you, but your anxious self is not your real self.

Perfectionism

I have been a perfectionist my entire life. I still am. I still struggle with the pressure that I put on myself every single day, but I've learned a lot about how to fight back against it.

Throughout high school, I expected perfection from myself in every aspect of my life. I didn't just need straight A's; I would feel a twinge of disappointment at anything less than 100%. I expected myself to be valedictorian. I expected myself to run varsity cross country and PR every single race. I wouldn't raise my hand in class if I weren't 100% sure that I had the right answer. I needed always to say the right thing, give the best advice, be funny but not be the center of attention. In my mind, I told myself that I was just trying to give 100% to everything that I did. But all I was really doing was putting everyone else in front of myself. No matter how tired or busy I was, I would always say yes to more things because resting was lazy, not spending all my free time studying was lazy, not being available 24/7 made me a terrible friend. I convinced myself that I could always have done better. After every test and every cross-country race, no matter how hard I studied or how hard I pushed myself, I needed to do better. For what, though? For who? Certainly no one else in my life expected those things from me. My mother begged me to get B's. She would gladly take a B in AP World History over seeing me sobbing and shaking in a panic attack on the kitchen floor twice a week. She would hold my head in her lap and tell me that it didn't need to be this way, she'd tell me how smart I was and how bright and witty and funny. My coach would always congratulate me after races, telling me how strong I looked. My friends would tell me that I had a big heart and gave incredible advice. No one cared about numbers. But it wasn't about an 89 vs. a 90 in history. It wasn't about a 23 minute 5k. It wasn't how many times I hung out with a particular friend. I was smart and strong and loving without quantifying those things in numbers.

Another major area of perfectionism-induced anxiety was how consumed I became with other people's opinions of me. I cannot tell you how many times I laid in my bed, my stomach clenching with anxiety, over saying the wrong thing. If I said a wrong answer in class, snapped at a friend, or got shot down by a boy, you could bet I spent the next week going over the situation again and again in my mind, cringing internally and beating myself up. Every conversation had to go exactly how I had previously planned it in my head, and if I didn't cater to everyone's needs and make everyone that I talked to feel heard and valued then I was a useless friend. Also, for each day, interaction, and relationship to be perfect, they all had to be happy to be perfect. Not every day is happy. Arguments are healthy in relationships. People are awkward and say the wrong thing and make people unhappy sometimes. That's a guarantee. You know what's not a guarantee? Always meeting all of your highest expectations of yourself.

This was the cycle of my life; I would make a mistake, be that failing a test, or saying the wrong thing to someone, and then spending the next week hating myself, beating myself up, and promising that I would do better next time. I would think through every possible detail of the situation and make a game plan for how to *never* let that mistake happen again. I hoped that eventually by process of elimination I would get to a point where I was making no more mistakes. Ever.

The primary element of my perfectionism was my need for everyone around me to see me as perfect. It was fine for everyone else to have problems and weaknesses, and I was always happy to help them with those things. But me? No. I could not. Anna Shutley did not have weaknesses. Anna Shutley had to be the best at everything, make no mistakes, never fail or quit or trip going up the stairs or flirt with the wrong person. Everyone else could, and I was never judgmental of others in that regard. They're all human, and make mistakes and have flaws and are still beautiful, intelligent people worthy of love. But not me. I was convinced that if I was not perfect, people would leave me. They would stop loving me and lose interest. Anytime I messed up I jeopardized all of my relationships. And again, no one told me I had to live like this. All of my friends and family give me so much unconditional love and support. But I, once again, believed that my worth was dependent upon my performance.

If any of this sounds familiar to you, here's my advice. Letting your worth depend on other people is the same concept as allowing the events of your day determine your happiness. All that matters is what you think of yourself. Are you the person you want to be? Are the things that you spend your time on making you happy? The thing is, no one cares as much as you think they do. No one is judging you as much as you think they are. Stop projecting your insecurities onto other people and convincing yourself that your friends are thinking the same things. Break out of the cycle of punishing yourself for your mistakes. Expecting yourself to be perfect in everything is impossible, unrealistic, and unhealthy. Life is truly not supposed to be this hard. We are all inherently flawed, but we are also all inherently *good.*

I still have to work hard to convince myself that none of the negative thoughts running through my head are true. I still struggle with needing myself to be outstanding in every aspect of my life. I'm starting to develop a better relationship with academics and with my self-confidence. And like my relationship with my mental health, it's always a process, always a journey, so embrace it for what it is.

Conclusion

So, here's the thing. This book is full of what I hope to be helpful advice. I am sure that your parents, teachers, family, and friends also give you a lot of really helpful advice. And maybe you are in therapy or working towards that milestone, or on medication. But at the end of the day, your depression is not going to magically disappear. There is no pill, no book, no exciting vacation, no college acceptance letter, no boy, and no friend that is going to come into your life and fix everything for you. The road to recovery from mental illness is hard as hell. I know that. But no one is going to walk that path for you and there are no shortcuts. At the end of the day, you have to decide that you want to get better. All of the advice in the world is not going to help you unless you stop just listening to it and start actually *living* it. There is a song by Kodaline called "What It Is", and it contains the lyrics "So you're standing in the parking lot of life, and you're trying to figure out your fate tonight....yeah, that's just the way it is. Nobody's gonna tell you how to live". I love the message in this song because it's true - no one can live your life for you, and no one is going to tell you the way that you need to live your life to recover. You have a support system, you know where you can start, and you have ideas about how to go about changing your life. Your future can be so much happier, more full of love and joy and passion and dedication than your present seems to be. You have a future that is worth fighting for, and worth changing for. You never asked to be afflicted by depression, so stop letting it be the deciding element of your life. Fight back. Fight back because you have thousands of Tuesdays left ahead of you. Thousands of days that everyone around you is going to take for granted and count down until they're over. Keep fighting because all those Tuesdays filled with happiness that you cannot currently fathom are waiting for you.

How to Parent a Child with Depression

Parenting a child with depression is extremely difficult. To watch your child suffer through an internal battle that you cannot fix is painful. Depression has no easy fix and please do not treat it as such. You cannot cure your child's mental illness with a positivity journal, or with this book or any other, or through denying the existence of their illness. You also cannot walk their road to recovery for them. You cannot get frustrated when they have a bad day or don't seem to be practicing their coping mechanisms. Be gentle with your child during their darker days, and be a positive encouragement and steady presence when they have the energy to be receptive to your advice.

Should my child be in therapy?

Some children, like myself, ask to go to therapy. Others need a nudge to realize its benefits. Either way, if your child is anywhere on the spectrum of suffering from depression, I could not recommend therapy enough. Having another adult figure in their life to talk to, receive advice from, and having a person who will provide professional counseling to a struggling child makes an enormous difference. That said, a counselor is legally obligated to tell you if your child is in danger (i.e., having thoughts or plans for self-harm or suicide), but if not, it is up to your child whether they want to discuss the details of their therapy sessions with you. Let this be their choice. Don't pry or make your child feel like they need to tell you. Again, this is not your journey. He/she will not fully recover until they can cope with their emotions on their own and process their thoughts. Therapy is also beneficial because it helps people who are unable to put into words or truly understand how they are feeling. When I would talk with my therapist, her questions would lead me to conclusions and realizations that I would never have come to on my own but were entirely accurate, and these realizations led to my significant

breakthroughs in therapy.

What if I cannot afford therapy?

Many employee health care and EAPs (Employee Assistance Programs) will cover a certain amount of

therapy sessions from specific counselors. You can contact your company human resources department for more

information.

Other options include

- Look for practices that offer a sliding fee scale

- Contact your faith organization for resources or support

- Call your local United Way information line for resources

What if my child is just overly dramatic?

"Sometimes the only reason I don't kill myself is because I don't want to do that to my family and I don't want to

die in shame. That's why I wish cancer upon myself so that I can leave peacefully and I'll leave feeling missed

instead of this. It has to get better. Please tell me that one day I won't feel like a shell with a black heart that no

longer beats. Every day is like walking on thin ice, and I am drowning and running out of reasons to try to swim".

"Dad was talking about how repelling off a cliff in California was the scariest thing he'd ever done and I was

about to agree when I remembered the nights that I still go through, lying in bed and crying and feeling so

worthless and trying to think of reasons not to kill myself and crying more when the list is so short and feeling

like I can't breathe and the voices in my head telling me how worthless I am. Those are the scariest".

These are excerpts from my journal that I kept my sophomore year of high school. This is how I felt. I

wrote the darkest parts of my heart out on these pages because I knew (ironically now) that no one would ever

read them. My mom initially did not think that I had a real issue. I have always been a dramatic person, and I had

frequent bouts of flopping down on the ground and wailing about my problems and making everything seem

worse than it was. If this is a recurring issue, don't tell your kid to knock it off or assume that they are simply

looking for attention. You don't know the darkest parts of their heart and chances are that they are probably hiding some of that from you. Give your child the benefit of the doubt and make sure that they are okay and if you suspect that they are not, please take action sooner rather than later.

Is this my fault? Did I parent him/her poorly?

On paper, I had no reason in the world to be depressed. I grew up in a happy and healthy nuclear family with financial stability. I have amazing, supportive parents with a healthy marriage and I got to go on lots of exciting vacations and adventures. I did very well in school, participated in sports, went to church every Sunday. I had friends. There was no reason for me to be depressed, and yet I was. Depression is a mental illness, and it can affect anyone. And while it is heartbreaking and painful that it is affecting your son or daughter, there is no one singular thing that you could have done to cause this.

I was afraid to tell my parents about my suicidal thoughts because I thought that they would be disappointed in me or believe that they had failed as parents and I didn't want them to believe that. No one wants their child to have suicidal thoughts, and no child wants to have them either. Having healthy communication without blame or fear of retribution is what high-schoolers with depression need from their parents. Provide this and never blame yourself.

Should I let my child skip school when they want to?

An occasional mental health day is needed. Don't be afraid to let them take one. But don't allow it become a pattern. As much as they may not feel like going to school, missing class is going to create more problems down the road. In addition, your child needs to practice functioning with depression; they may not have the best day if you force them to go to school, but they are forced to interact with people, be productive, and put their depression on the back burner for a little while, which can prevent it from becoming consuming. Again, when I was in a very, very bad place, my mom would let me have a mental health day. However, she would call in from work and stay home to make sure that I was staying safe, and she would require that I spent some time journaling, reflecting on my feelings and attempting to utilize the coping mechanisms that I learned in therapy. Do not let them lock themselves in their room or bathroom. If you feel that your child is in actual imminent danger, call an ambulance. Get them to the emergency room. You may think that this is a dramatic reaction or that you are misusing the hospital resources, but it is *always* better to err on the side of caution, especially if your child's life is on the line.

My child is going to therapy and taking medication, so why is nothing improving?

Again, the road to recovery from depression is not a steady uphill line. There will be failures with every victory, setbacks that accompany every breakthrough. It took me years of therapy and antidepressants before my mood, behavior, and mental illness changed significantly. The most that you can do is be a rock and a refuge for your child, a safe place where they can share their emotions with you uncensored and know that you love them unconditionally, no matter what their recovery process looks like. Many factors can also be influencing a seemingly slow recovery process, such as the age of your child, their hormones, etc. Talk with their therapist if you have concerns like this.

Why won't my child be honest about his/her feelings?

When your child comes to you with a problem or wants to talk, start every conversation by asking them what they want from you. Ask if they want advice or if they want you to just listen. This will allow them to tell you what they need and prevent you from feeling like your words of advice are going unheard.

"And sometimes she'll get sad and she'll share it with you. Not for you to cheer her up. Just be quiet and feel it with her. Because sometimes she needs to feel it to let it go, but she doesn't want to feel so alone". - J. M. Storm

Depression sucks. And there will be days when their heart feels like it's tied to an anvil and like they can barely stay afloat. Only they can process these emotions, and sometimes they just need to tell you what is on their heart so that they know you understand how bad it is. Don't try to fix it, because you can't. Just be what they need, and they will come to you for what they need.

Also, never, ever mention to your child the cost of their therapy sessions or make them feel like those sessions or the price of their medications are a waste of money. No depressed child needs that added weight or worry. If the financial aspect of the therapy is a problem, there are many options such as insurance, EAP, or school-covered counseling sessions.

What if I know what behaviors are worsening my child's depression?

If you see dangerous patterns emerging from certain behaviors or interactions with certain people, do not

be afraid to voice your opinion. I cannot promise that your child will always obey your advice or that they will

immediately understand your position and argument, but it's likely that they will come around eventually.

References

Domonell, Kristen. "Endorphins and the Truth About Runner's High." Life by Daily Burn, Life
    by Daily Burn, 14 July 2016, dailyburn.com/life/fitness/what-are-endorphins-runners-high/.

Fischman, Josh. "How Your Smartphone Messes with Your Brain-and Your Sleep." Scientific
    American Blog Network, 20 May 2014, blogs.scientificamerican.com/observations/how-your-
    smartphone-messes-with-your-brain-and-your-sleep/.

Generalized Anxiety Disorder (GAD). Anxiety and Depression Association of America,
    ADAA, adaa.org/understanding-anxiety/generalized-anxiety-disorder-gad#.

Symptoms. Anxiety and Depression Association of America, ADAA, adaa.org/understanding-
    anxiety/panic-disorder-agoraphobia/symptoms#.

Made in the USA
Lexington, KY
26 July 2018